the guide to owning

# Central American Cichlids

Richard F. Stratton

T.F.H. Publications, Inc.
One TFH Plaza
Third and Union Avenues
Neptune City, NJ 07753

This book has been published with the intent to provide accurate and authoritative information in regard to the subject matter within. While every precaution has been taken in preparation of this book, the publisher and author assume no responsibility for errors or omissions. Neither is any liability assumed for damages resulting from the use of the information herein.

ISBN 0-7938-2203-3

Printed and bound in the United States of America

Printed and Distributed by T.F.H. Publications, Inc.
Neptune City, NJ

# Contents

# Real Cichlids!

It is with tongue firmly implanted in cheek that I refer to Central American cichlids as "real cichlids." It is somewhat presumptuous to refer to any group of cichlids as the "real McCoy." That is because cichlids have become so popular among tropical fish hobbyists that different groups of cichlidophiles are advocates for different groups of cichlids from different parts of the world. In fact, there is much good-natured intramural warfare about which group is the prettiest or the most interesting to keep.

Cichlids have become among the most popular families of fishes to keep because they are colorful and, more importantly, they provide some form of parental care for the young. That is, they protect the eggs and keep them from being eaten by predators, and they care for them by keeping them aerated and clean. They even pick out bad eggs that don't look right so that they don't spread the infection (fungal or bacterial) to the other eggs. After the eggs hatch and the fry are free swimming, the cichlid parents cooperate in herding the youngsters to food and in protecting them from potential predators. Some cichlid parents even chew up food and spit it out into the cloud of fry. They also use their anal fins as brooms to stir up sedimentary fragments that might provide food for the young. In nearly every way, they are quite reminiscent of mother hens, except that the father provides care, too. In fact, they go a step further than a mother hen in that several species secrete specialized body slime for nourishing the young. This provides a sort of "milk" as a first or supplementary food for their offspring.

In spite of all of this tender care for the young that cichlids display, for many years they enjoyed favor among only a select few advanced aquarists. That was mainly because many of the relatively few species

One of the greatest attractions of cichlid ownership in general and ownership of Central American cichlids in particular is to be able to observe parent fish interacting with their fry; a Midas cichlid (*Cichlasoma citrinellum*) parent and fry group is shown here.

available tended to be too large for home aquariums and also were quite aggressive, especially when spawning time arrived. In addition, the fishes uprooted plants, especially at spawning time, and tended to shred them even after they had been uprooted. Other than being too big for the aquarium and being inclined to murder their tankmates and destroy plants, cichlids were really nice! Often those eccentrics among us who kept them maintained them in very large homemade tanks. We decorated the tanks with rockwork in order to prevent the devastation of the plants. We kept only cichlids in those tanks, and we kept them according to the level of aggression of the different species.

Two things happened to make cichlids widely popular among nearly all advanced aquarists. One was that larger tanks and better filtration methods were developed by manufacturers, and the other was the importation of the endemic cichlids of the rift lakes of Africa. These fishes were wildly colorful, and many of them supplied the movement all over the tank that is sometimes lacking from cichlids that have a more lurking type of demeanor. In the resulting mania for "African cichlids," by which aquarists and shopkeepers nearly always meant cichlids from the rift lakes of Africa, the original cichlids from Central and South America were eclipsed to a certain extent. So were some of the cichlids from West Africa, which had been part of the original contingent of cichlids kept by earlier hobbyists.

Besides color and the fact that there were so many species, the newcomers were popular because of their variety, as they had evolved to fill niches that would normally be filled by species of other families. That meant that many species had odd shapes and quite interesting habits. One reason for this situation was that cichlids were able to colonize the African rift lakes without much competition, and there were many niches for them to fill, given time to adapt. However, it should be noted that a somewhat similar, if less dramatic, situation exists in Central America. Cichlids were among the first fishes to colonize the new freshwater areas that were made available when the Central American land mass was elevated. They dominate the Central American fish fauna in terms of species in the same way that they dominate the African rift lakes. What is more, they are real cichlids!

I use the term "real cichlids" in a playful

The South American discusfishes (*Symphysodon* species) immediately come to mind as cichlids that provide nourishment for the fry from their own bodies, but in some Central American species as well the fry feed from the parents' bodies, although not to the same extent.

way, as I am a bona fide fan of nearly all cichlids, and people who know me know that. But I was not the first to use the term. A well known ichthyologist (who will stay anonymous to protect the guilty!) was to my knowledge, the first to use it, in a talk he gave to a large fish club meeting. The use of the term evoked applause (as well as groans), for many old-time cichlidophiles had never fully accepted the new imports from Africa, as they didn't like the fact that so many of them were mouthbrooders and that they were fast-swimming and weasel-like, as was the case of many of the mbuna of Lake Malawi. Some dyed-in-the-wool cichlidophiles of the old school simply refused to even keep these "aliens," although they were—and still are—very popular with the general public.

Others of us took the plunge and kept many of the newcomers, but the experience solidified the respect we had for the old type that we previously had experience with. Besides, as mentioned earlier, the Central American cichlids had specializations of their own and tended to dominate the fish faunas of their respective areas. For that reason and others there has been renewed interest in the Central American forms.

## WHAT IS A CICHLID?

At this point, it is worth reviewing just what it is we are talking about here. Most of us learn to recognize cichlids, but we are not always sure how we do it. All cichlids are members of the family Cichlidae (pronounced sick-lid-dee). The type specimen

African cichlids like this colorful *Cyrtocara moorii* from Lake Malawi form a cichlid specialty group that rivals and in some ways surpasses the popularity of Central American cichlids, but both groups have much in common.

for the family is a South American cichlid, *Cichla ocellaris.*

There are believed to be about 1200 species in the family, with new ones being described every year. Members of the family are found mostly in North and Central America, South America, Africa and some outlying islands, including Madagascar; two species are known from southern India. Only one species is native to the United States, but a number of non-native species have been released in Florida waters. Those introduced species have been a disaster for Florida's natural ichthyofauna, as they have out-competed many native species. There are also non-native cichlids in a warm springs area in southern Nevada and in the lower reaches of the Colorado River, and at least a couple of species in the Salton Sea and the surrounding waters.

Cold water is a definite barrier to cichlids, so at least they are not going to take over the entire country. Incidentally, although this book's title derives from the fact that it is devoted primarily to Central American cichlids, it covers North American species as well, since it lists both the one species native to the United States and a number of species native to Mexico.

It is interesting to note that cichlids are secondary freshwater fishes, meaning that it is believed that they evolved from marine ancestors. This is interesting, because modern bony fishes are believed to have evolved in fresh water and then to have moved to conquer the oceans (or at least to fill in the niches not taken by sharks and other primitive forms!). So the cichlid ancestor is thought to have been one of those marine fish returning to carve out a

*Etroplus suratensis,* one of the very few Asiatic cichlid species.

place for itself in fresh waters. In any case, the history of the family helps explain why many species are able to survive in salty water; some cichlids, in fact, do extend their range into parts of the ocean.

Cichlids are modern fishes, with spiny fins and modern structures. The species of the family have been shown to be monophyletic (descended from a common ancestor) by Dr. Melanie L. J. Stiassny, so the family Cichlidae, as large as it is, will remain intact. Since cichlids have been the object of much recent taxonomic work, many of the scientific names have been revised, usually involving a change in the generic name. These changes reflect a better understanding of the species and the relationships among them.

Cichlid keepers get so they can tell on sight whether a given fish is a cichlid, but they are not always sure how they do it. Besides certain internal structures, cichlids are diagnosed primarily by the single nostril on each side of the snout. Since that is what

we have also, it may seem perfectly normal; however, most fish species have two nostrils on each side, with the water running through one opening and out the other. The single nostril on each side is a recent innovation for fishes. The nostrils operate like a syringe, taking in water for olfactory analysis and expelling it. This feature is shared by the damselfishes (Pomacentridae) of the tropical seas, and cichlids are more closely related to them than to any other family. However, cichlids are also closely allied to wrasses, parrotfishes, and surfperches.

Although some cichlids, such as the discus and the angel, have an exotic form, most species are more generalized, looking like a "classic" fish. The most colorful species are concentrated in Lake Malawi, but there are some real stunners all over the world. (Cichlid people become so enamored of the various different and complex behavior patterns of different species that they often keep some plain-looking ones and, what's more, they do so without shame!) Although the single nostril on each side of the snout is enough to distinguish cichlids from all other freshwater species, there are other external structures that denote the family Cichlidae. For example, the pectoral fins are approximately even with the ventral (sometimes called pelvic) fins. This is one of the signs of modern (recently evolved) fish species. One of the hallmarks of a cichlid that is not so apparent externally is the presence of teeth in the jaws and in the throat. Many other fish families have one or the other but not both. That feature, among others, was what helped Dr. Stiassny to group cichlids with damselfishes, wrasses, parrotfishes, and surfperches in the superfamily Labridae. This feature also is among those that scientists believe has made cichlids able to invade newly opened areas of fresh water and pretty much dominate. They can evolve the jaw teeth for one purpose, such as grasping, and the pharyngeal teeth (i.e. teeth in the throat) can evolve for grinding. The development of the jaws themselves is unique. Without getting technical here, the structure of the jaws allows for much variation on a theme. This helps in the relatively rapid evolution of species to fill different feeding niches in the same environment.

Generally speaking, cichlids are adapted to slow-moving waters and for lakes, and

Having only two nostrils, one on each side of the snout, instead of the four nostrils that most other fishes have, is a character shared by cichlids and related species, as evidenced in this bumpheaded male synspilus and his mate.

their swimming ability is finely tuned more for precision than for speed. However, some species are exceptions to this, as they have evolved to be open-water predators that chase down their prey.

The other feature that helps cichlids do well in lake habitats is that they care for their young. Other fishes, for the most part, depend on the production of large amounts of eggs to compensate for the fact that no parental care is involved. There are two essential requirements for the survival of fish eggs: first, general cleanliness of the eggs to protect them from bacterial and fungal infections and, second, protection from predation. Other species hide the eggs up rivers or streams where there are the fewest predators. The clear currents of streams also help to keep the eggs clean and oxygenated. But such strategies tie the species that utilize them to spawning seasonally, and it makes them dependent upon upper streams or rivers for spawning. They are thus not well suited to a lake environment.

Cichlids, then, have the advantage, most particularly in a lake. The parents care for the eggs and for the young, keeping them clean and protecting them from predators. There is much variation in how this is done. In some species, the parents pair up, then clean a rock and lay the eggs upon it. They fan the eggs to keep them clean and well aerated. At the same time, they drive off fishes and other potential predators that might eat the eggs. There is much variety on this theme, too, as some cichlid species utilize caves. Others use movable platforms, such as the leaves from certain trees, and they move the eggs from place to place for the best protection. Other species dig underground chambers, while still

Synpilus exhibits typical egg-tending behavior for a substrate-spawning Central American cichlid.

THE GUIDE TO OWNING CENTRAL AMERICAN CICHLIDS

others spawn in the empty shells of mollusks.

The other method that cichlids utilize for caring for their brood is mouthbrooding of the eggs. That is, the female lays the eggs, they are fertilized, and the female picks up the eggs and incubates them in her mouth. Again, there is much variation along this theme, too. In some species, both the male and female help brood the eggs. In at least a few species, the male does the job. In the species *Chromidotilapia guentheri* the male broods the eggs, and the female guards him. After the hatched fry are released, both parents share in their protection. In some species, the female broods only five to ten eggs, but she broods them for such an extended period of time that the fry are miniature adults when they emerge.

Anyway, you get the idea: there are many variations to each style of caring for the eggs. Many cichlidophiles prefer the substrate-spawning species to the mouthbrooding ones because they like to see the cooperation and coordination of care between the parents; however, this behavior is not something that is always absent from mouthbrooding cichlids. Both systems are extremely successful, and it is difficult to gauge one as being better than the other. Nearly all of the cichlids of Lake Malawi and Lake Victoria are mouthbrooders, but the substrate-spawning cichlids of Lake Tanganyika successfully compete with the mouthbrooders there. And some of the most successful cichlids in the world are substrate spawners.

## SCIENTIFIC NAMES

Cichlid keepers should become familiar with scientific names, because popular names are often unreliable. For example, a species may be called a Texas cichlid in one part of the United States and a Rio Grande perch in another, and it might be called a pearl cichlid in England and something altogether different in Australia. Even the scientific names can be a problem, as they can change from time to time; right now, in fact, many names of cichlid species—Central American species definitely included—are in a state of flux. Still, nearly all serious cichlid fanciers try to learn (and keep up with the changes in) the scientific names of their favorite fishes. It's not difficult to get used to using scientific names, so let me briefly review how they fit into the scheme of classifying living things like fishes.

There are several levels of classification in biology. The most inclusive level is the kingdom. There are five kingdoms presently accepted by all biologists: Monera, Protista, Fungi, Plantae, and Animalia, corresponding, respectively, to: bacteria, single-celled organisms with nuclei, fungi (including mushrooms), plants, and animals. The levels of classification are the following: kingdom, phylum, class, order, family, genus, and species.

We can see that each group is less and less inclusive; that is, it is more restrictive as to the number of species it includes. Thus, if we take the human species, we are in the animal kingdom, the phylum of chordates (Chordata), the class of mammals (Mammalia), the order of primates (which includes monkeys, lemurs, and apes), the family Hominidae (of which we are the only surviving members, although there are several fossil species), the genus *Homo,* and the species *sapiens.*

This system of classification has served very well ever since its inception. Of course, scientists tinker with it a bit to meet their needs. They will thus utilize groupings in between the classifications. For example, there are subphyla and superfamilies. Such classifications are merely a convenience, a way of dealing with animals that fit in the system, but it is realistic to consider some very similar animals (or whatever) in "superfamilies," for example. These would be animals that are too dissimilar to be placed in the same family yet have some common traits that tie the families together. In the case of cichlids, they are grouped with the marine families Pomacanthidae, Labridae, Scaridae, and Embiotocidae to form the superfamily Labridae. It is just a matter of stretching and bending the classification system to accommodate the fact that there are often no clear distinctions between categories. After all, the whole classification scheme is simply an artificial construct of humankind to enable it to better understand the universe. The same could be said of certain features of physics and mathematics.

As I said, we are primarily interested in the names of species. They consist of two names, the genus (or generic) name and the species (or specific) name. Thus we are *Homo sapiens.* That means "wise man." (In Latin, the adjective follows the noun.) Of course, it is nice to be able to do the naming, as we can give ourselves a good name! Notice that both ends of the name are in italics and that the generic name starts off with a capital letter, whereas the specific name does not. The popular press commonly ignores convention by not capitalizing the first letter of the generic name and in capitalizing the first letter of the specific name and also by not italicizing either name, even when italics are available.

With most Central American cichlids, the generic name has always been *Cichlasoma,* but therein lies a story of some controversy. If the reader will remain steadfast for just a moment, we will review that quickly and then get to the fish and how to keep them!

*Cichlasoma* is a scientific name that has been used for many years to cover cichlids all the way from southern South America to Central America. It has been known all along by ichthyologists who specialize in cichlids that a diverse group of animals, too diverse to be included in one genus, has been covered by that classification. One temporary solution by the great ichthyologist C. Tate Regan, was to split the Central American cichlids up into groups that he called "sections." Other ichthyologists have generally treated those sections as subgeneric groupings. Although ichthyologists who took a special interest in cichlids acknowledged that work needed to be done on the genus *Cichlasoma,* none was inclined, apparently, to tackle the great amount of work involved in splitting up this group of over eighty species. Then in 1983 Dr.

*Satanoperca jurupari,* a South American mouthbrooding cichlid species that is an even more active digger than its Central American relatives.

Sven Kullander began the work that so many had avoided for so long. He restricted the genus *Cichlasoma* to just twelve species in South America. This, in effect, orphaned all the other *Cichlasoma* species. The question then became what to call the other species until Kullander or someone else did the work to break these various *Cichlasoma* up into different genera. One solution was to use the next available name that had been used for *Cichlasoma,* which was *Heros.* The problem with that was that the name *Heros* was soon utilized for a distinct group of cichlids, making the other cichlids of the *Cichlasoma* group once again orphaned. The next available name is *Herichthys.* (The "available" names are generic names that were once used for cichlids of the *Cichlasoma* group but were used after *Cichlasoma* had been used. For that reason, *Cichlasoma* had priority. However, once *Cichlasoma* was restricted to just the species in South America, the junior synonyms, such as *Heros* and

*Herichthys,* could be used. *Heros* had priority, but it has been restricted to the *C. severum*-like fishes of South America, so *Herichthys* is now available.) The trouble is that *Herichthys* is very likely to be restricted to the group of cichlids that the Texas cichlid belongs to. That means that we will once again be looking for another name. For that reason, for purposes of this book I propose to retain *Cichlasoma* for most species, but I will use the "sections" of Regan, as they are presently applied, in parentheses, as these names very likely will eventually become the generic names for the species so indicated.

The fact is that we are not in bad company here, as many ichthyologists still use *Cichlasoma* in the scientific literature, waiting for all the revisions to be made and for general acceptance of them before switching names. This is conservative, and it is the easy way out. And those are good enough reasons for me!

# A Tank for Central American Cichlids

## TANK SIZE

The things that you have to give some thought to when you've decided to set up a tank for Central American cichlids are pretty much the same things you have to think of when choosing a tank for fishes of any kind. First, of course, you have to take into account your own personal situation—such things as how much money you have, how much space you're able to devote to the aquarium, how much weight your floors will bear, and your own individual tastes in tank shapes and materials. There is not much sense, for example, in your planning to set up an aquarium to house some of the big bruisers among Central American cichlids if all you have room for is a 10-gallon (38 liter) tank. A tank of 20 gallons (76 liters) in capacity is about the lower limit called for in keeping Central American cichlids, even the smaller ones.

You also have to take into consideration how the tank is going to be used. Is it going to be set up as a community tank, or will you use it solely or primarily as a one-pair-at-a-time breeding tank? For a number of species you can get by with a 20-gallon unit as a breeding tank, but for a community aquarium nothing much smaller than a 50-gallon (190 liters) should be used.

Nowadays the trend is toward larger and larger tanks, and they can be pure delight if you're able to accommodate and maintain them. The first cichlid community tank I ever saw was a 50-gallon, and I saw it at a time when a tank that size was considered very large by home aquarium standards. The tank was jammed with really big fishes, and by today's standards it was woefully under-filtered, with just a few air-powered inside box filters doing all the filtration work. The fishes themselves were doing

A Central American cichlid (*Cichlasoma fenestratum*) at home in the rockwork of its large tank.

very well, but that was only because the owner of the tank was a master aquarist who had enough experience to head off trouble before it could start doing real damage. He knew what he was doing, and he made all of the right water changes and filter medium changes; he also knew just what and, even more importantly, how much to feed. So he could run his tank more or less on the edge of danger. The rest of us, however, need more equipment and less courting of disaster; we need much more wiggle room than he allowed himself.

In a cichlid tank, another big point that you have to deal with is the aggression level. The cichlid community tank mentioned above, for example, employed a lot of rockwork as places of refuge into and around which pursued or otherwise harassed fishes in the tank could dart and dive to escape their tormentors. Coarse and fine gravel mixed together formed the tank's substrate.

The best rocks to use are those of volcanic origin, pumice being an especially good choice because of its relatively light weight and its ease of being worked and shaped. Some other rocks are capable of leaching toxic substances into the tank and should be avoided. Slate and shale are non-toxic old standbys and often have the advantage of being available in slabs, which allows for the construction of cavelike structures of the type many cichlids love. Better to be safe than sorry in erecting your rockwork, so don't set up any combination with dangerous overhangs that can come crashing down to smash the bottom or sides of the tank. You can use the same rubbery silicone-base adhesive that glues an all-glass tank's sides together to help fasten rocks into permanent positions.

The artificial rocks sold commercially have two other advantages in addition to being non-toxic. They look good and, because they are hollow, are comparatively very light in weight. The latter is a pretty big consideration if you ever have to remove all the rockwork, as you might find yourself having to do if you want to net an individual fish or two. Cichlids are masters of the maze that rockwork creates and can be almost impossible to catch while there are rocky hiding places into which they can duck.

Although cichlids in general are notorious for their tendency to reduce all plantings in their tanks to just so much uproooted vegetative matter, some plants can be kept in cichlid tanks. A lot depends on how much effort you are willing to put into trying to outwit those of your cichlids that are dedicated plant uprooters. One trick is to put the plants into pots instead of planting them in the gravel, using coarse pebbles over the gravel in which the plants are rooted—but if your cichlids (or a particular one among them) are bound and determined to turn your rooted plants into floaters, they'll probably succeed in the end. Many cichlidkeepers do without plants entirely in an effort to save themselves annoyance. The most they keep are floating plants, such as water sprite, duckweed, and anacharis. Both the water sprite and anacharis are often used planted instead of floating, but in such cases they are much more easily uprooted by the cichlids. Duckweed serves as a food for some cichlids, although it's not always certain whether the fish are eating the duckweed for its own sake or for the small animals, crustaceans in particular, that live in it; duckweed also has value as a shade-provider, and it multiplies very quickly.

## FILTRATION

Filtration can be as simple as a few inside-the-tank filters or as complex as a series of outside-the-tank compound filters, including such exotic ones as algae filters and trickle filters. The fact is that many people who keep Central American cichlids make use of either inside box or foam (sponge) filters, especially if they are trying to breed their stock. The filters are changed frequently, and so is the water. Also, good aquarium practices are followed in managing the water. For that reason, someone with the simplest of systems can outdo a more careless aquarist with exotic filtration.

Nevertheless, hobbyists who simply want to keep a community tank of Central American cichlids will very likely want to make use of some of the more powerful filter systems. Let's make a quick survey of what is available.

## TYPES OF FILTRATION

One big aspect of water filtration is to remove from the water the small pieces of solid matter that float around in it, for the most part uneaten foodstuffs and fish wastes and decaying vegetation. That type is referred to as mechanical filtration. Another type of filtration, called biological filtration, attempts to use bacterial action to break down the metabolites that are excreted by the fish. It is much more important than simple mechanical filtration, because it is what makes the water livable for the fish. A third type of filtration, chemical filtration, seeks to remove dissolved substances from the water. Its most common agent, activated carbon, is used in conjunction with mechanical and biological filtration systems.

## MECHANICAL FILTRATION

Mechanical filtration makes the water look good and, provided that the filter medium used is cleaned or replaced often enough, also reduces the quantity of pollution-causing elements in the tank. Mechanical filters also serve to at least a small extent as biological filters, as the beneficial bacteria that populate biological filters will lodge in mechanical filters as well, although in much lesser numbers.

The major mechanical filtration devices on the market today do a very good job of removing solid waste particles from aquarium water. The most popular units powerful enough to do a good job on a large cichlid tank are the hang-on-the-tank power filters and the so-called canister filters. Both types are available in

**Canister filters can be kept out of sight in cabinets underneath the aquarium.**

numerous different models, including models that provide biological and, through the use of activated carbon, chemical filtration. In their function as mechanical filters, both the hanging power filters and the canister filters draw water from the aquarium and then process that water through a filter medium or media to screen out particulates before returning the water to the aquarium. The major functional difference between the two types is that in the canister filter the water is pumped through the filter medium under pressure, whereas in the hanging power filter it doesn't have to be. Canisters can be situated away from (usually hidden in a cabinet underneath) the aquarium instead of having to hang from its rim, and many hobbyists consider this to be an advantage. Canister filters in general provide a greater volume of filter space than hang-ons and also are more adaptable to having useful attachments added to them, but they are more expensive.

Less powerful mechanical filters are air-operated inside-the-tank box filters, perforated or slotted plastic containers that are placed into the aquarium itself and filter the aquarium's water through layers of fibrous material, usually in tandem with the use of activated carbon. Unlike canister filters and other power filters, inside-the-tank box filters don't contain motors to move water and therefore require the use of an air pump or a small submersible water pump

(power head) to circulate the aquarium's water through them. But they are easily moved from tank to tank, that feature being of potential use in helping to seed a new tank with a colony of nitrifying bacteria. They also are relatively inexpensive, although if you choose to run them from a power head or one of the more expensive air pumps their costs will quickly start to mount up.

There are variations on the inside-the-tank theme here, as there are submersible inside-the-tank power filters on the market also; these filters can be either primarily mechanical or primarily biological. Inside-the-tank power filters are only occasionally used by cichlid specialists, as cichlid people love lots of aeration, and the inside power filters don't provide it

## Diatomaceous Earth Filters

Diatomaceous earth is composed of sediments made up of the shells of ancient diatoms, single-celled algae encased in clear silica, much like glass. The tiny pores in the silica are less than a micron (a micron is .00004 of an inch, a millionth of a meter) across, so the material makes an excellent filtration medium.

Diatomaceous earth filters are strictly mechanical filters and provide no biological filtration. They should not be used as permanent filters. Nevertheless, they make the water so clear that the fish seem as if they were suspended in air; they are best suited to occasional use in a tank in which the water clarity is not up to your standards.

Although diatomaceous earth filters in normal use are strictly mechanical, a number of manufacturers offer the option of a medium that consists partly of diatomaceous earth and partly of activated carbon, thereby providing chemical filtration as well.

## BIOLOGICAL FILTERS

### Undergravel Filters

The most familiar biological filter is the one that has been a workhorse aquarium filter for many years now, the undergravel filter. Undergravel filters are called undergravel filters because they—get this—are placed under aquarium gravel. They consist generally of a flat plastic plate into which small perforations or slits have been machined to allow passage of water. Gravel, neither too coarse nor too fine, is placed to a depth of a few inches over the filter plate. Attached to the filter plate is an upright tube that can be attached to an air pump or a power head. The function of the air or water pump is to induce a partial vacuum under the filter plate, thereby causing water from the upper levels of the aquarium to descend through the gravel and then rise upward through the filter tube back into the tank. The water going through the gravel brings oxygen to the aerobic bacteria living in it, which bacteria convert the fish waste product ammonia into successively less toxic nitrogenous compounds.

Unfortunately, Central American cichlids can cause problems with undergravel filters. Although it may not happen often, even the smallest Central American cichlids can dig holes clear down to the filter plate of the undergravel filter. This completely compromises the filter's efficiency. Water follows the path of least resistance, and that least resistance is for the water to go down through the filter plate at places at which there is no gravel. Since the object of the undergravel filter is to pass the water through the gravel where the nitrifying bacteria are resident, not through the bare filter plate where the bacteria are not, the cichlids' digging messes up the filtration system.

Fortunately, this problem can be circumvented. A layer of gravel, a little over half of the total quantity of gravel to be used, can be placed on the filter plate. Then

*Cichlasoma guttulatum* **male after having spit out the substrate taken in while he was performing a little excavation work within his territory.**

plastic screening is placed over that layer, and then the remainder of the gravel is placed over the screening. That way the cichlids can't dig down past the screening, so the filter is always functioning.

A different problem with the under-gravel filter is that it leads to a build-up of debris within the filter medium (the gravel), and the accumulated debris tends to create dead spots that block the passage of water. One way to get around this problem is through the use of a gravel vacuum in conjunction with your periodic partial water changes; several different types are sold in aquarium stores.

Another approach is to use a reverse-flow undergravel filter. This involves running the water down what would normally be the lift tube and passing the water up through the gravel. An important point here is that the water must be filtered before being sent down beneath the gravel, the object being to keep the particulate matter out of the biological filter. This way the gravel tends to stay clear of debris almost indefinitely. Since cichlids tend to be large (and messy), the gravel should still be vacuumed regularly, but you don't have to be quite as conscientious as with the regular undergravel filter. Of course, the undergravel filter is not the only biological filter. There are others, such as the trickle filter and the fluidized bed filter, but they are all more strictly biological; they won't double as mechanical filters to anywhere near the same degree as the old standby under-

gravel filter. But some of them are even more efficient biological filters than the undergravel device, so you may want to consider one of them, particularly if you are keeping fish species for which you have to alter the pH and hardness of the water. If you use one or more of these devices, you won't have to make as many partial water changes and therefore won't have to do as much doctoring of your replacement water.

### Trickle Filters

The biological filters known as trickle filters are known also as wet/dry filters. Such filters have their basis in two facts: first, it takes biological filtration to keep water in truly good enough shape for our fishes; second, the bacteria required for such filtration are most efficient when they have access to lots of oxygen. Trickle filters spread the water out and give it plenty of surface area to spread over, which allows for good gas exchange. Different designs of these filters are simply different ways to achieve the same purpose that undergravel filters and other biological filters are intended for: to provide lots of oxygen and living space for the groups of desirable bacteria that break down deadly ammonia into the slightly less toxic nitrite and the nitrite into the much less harmful nitrate. Other bacteria can break down the nitrate, too, but those bacteria are anaerobic types; anaerobes do not need oxygen and in fact are killed by it, so in the long run it has been easier (at least in aquariums) to devise filters that provide oxygen for the aerobic bacteria than it has been to safely culture the anaerobic bacteria needed to break down nitrate.

Trickle filtration uses something called a sump, a sort of reservoir to hold a quantity of water that gets circulated back and forth between the aquarium and the sump. The sump is the "wet" part of the filter. The "dry" part is the filter medium or media over and through which the water is trickled. (Obviously "dry" here doesn't have the usual meaning of dry and is simply aquaristic cant meaning "wet but not fully submersed.")

Most currently offered trickle filter systems use spiky plastic spheres or plastic matting as the medium or media. Water is sprayed (by a spray bar) through the air over the filter medium or media and allowed to trickle down into the sump. The water is consequently very well aerated and, since it is also well spread out over the medium, there is a tremendous surface area for beneficial bacteria to populate and over which gas exchange can take place. It is important to keep light out of the sump to prevent the growth of algae that will compete with the bacteria. Hence the container that holds the medium often is dark-colored to inhibit light penetration, or the chamber itself may fit into a dark compartment.

One of the big advantages of the trickle filter is that the media don't have to be changed. This is true, however, only if you use a pre-filter, a mechanical screening component to keep debris out of the biomedia. The pre-filter should be easy to get to for cleaning or replacement during regular maintenance sessions. Many trickle filters also have a thick foam block to give the water a final filtering before it is pumped back into the aquarium. These blocks should be cleaned thoroughly or replaced on a regular basis.

### Fluidized Bed Filters

Less complicated than trickle filters are the fluidized bed filters, also called fluidized sand or just plain sand filters. Relatively new to the aquarium field even though the technology has been used in water treatment plants for a number of years, a fluidized bed system consists of many, perhaps millions, of pieces of sand that are kept continuously whirling around in a matrix of aquarium water by jets of water powered by a built-in pump. The grains of sand provide an enormous surface area for the beneficial bacteria to colonize, so fluidized bed filters have very high biological filtration powers. Additionally, the filter's efficiency is enhanced by the fact that the constant movement of the sand medium sloughs off overly thick growths of older bacteria on the individual grains of sand, allowing nutrients and oxygen to get through to newer and more productive layers.

Fluidized bed filters can be used in line with other filtration systems or set up separately with their own pumps and pre-filters. However used, fluidized bed filters are efficient and low-maintenance units—and it's fun to watch the sand grains swirl around.

Today's aquarium hobbyists are able to choose items of equipment that both look good and serve well in providing for the biological requirements of the fishes.

## ROTATING CONTACTORS

Rotating contactors, also called biowheels and water wheels, are another relatively new development on the aquarium market even though they've been around for a while in water treatment technology. They consist of a cylinder of highly porous and light material arranged in ridges around an axis that can rotate between two supports. Aquarium water poured or sprayed onto the cylinder (or, in the case of rotating contactors mounted onto outside power filters, with the "fins" of the contactor partially submersed in the stream of water being returned to the tank) causes it to rotate and thereby keep its surface continuously saturated by the water. (Lots of aquarium water carrying food for the beneficial bacteria plus lots of oxygen to which the saturated cylinder is exposed equals lots of biological filtration.)

### Other Filters

There are other filters on the market, some basically mechanical and some primarily biological and some purely chemical, some very simple and some very complicated, some of demonstrable utility and some (such as the algal turf scrubbers) still being experimented with. Among those that have proved their worth I'd list the sponge, or foam, filters, which in general share most of the advantages of the inside box filter and are even better than box filters in fry-rearing tanks. Unfortunately, sponge filters are less suitable for use in tanks given over to Central American cichlids, particularly the larger and more aggressive species; the cichlids can abuse the filters, biting pieces off and generally punishing them, often making the filter completely inoperative by pulling the foam piece off the rest of the filter.

## WATER CHANGES

As has already been noted, filtration and water changes go hand-in-hand for keeping the water in which your fishes live livable. Even with the best of filtration systems, you still have to make periodic water changes—and the exact method you employ in making those water changes depends to a certain extent on the type of water you have.

Basically, it all depends on whether you have to soften or harden. The easiest is if you have soft water and you want to keep hard-water fishes. All you have to do then is to buy salts that contain the minerals for reproducing such water. They are sold commercially in fish stores. Just follow the directions on the package.

It is a tougher proposition with hard water going to soft, but one method is to utilize peat moss in the filters. If possible, get to know some killifish people in your area, as they are the masters of the alchemy of peat moss. Killifish people simply dump peat moss onto the bottom of their tanks (after boiling it and processing it), because they don't have to worry about the tiny amounts of excrement their tiny fish will put out. In our case, it is different. Even the smallest Central American cichlid is too big to ignore in that respect, and besides, the cichlids are going to be around for a lot longer than the killies, which are basically short-lived animals. The peat moss can be placed in a mesh bag and replaced periodically. Killifish people will tell you how it should be boiled and soaked in water many times before actually being used, but this is not really necessary. Many claims are made for peat moss, from softening the water to adding desirable hormones. There is much folklore to this material, and it can be difficult to separate the whimsy from the whamsy, but peat moss has many loyal users among aquarists, and it must be admitted that the keeping of fish is as much an art as a science.

A more scientific, if more expensive, approach is to utilize a reverse osmosis device. These devices produce water that is almost completely pure of minerals, organic compounds, and metals. In fact, the water must be mixed with at least some of your tap water, for it is simply too soft for any fish.

Another alternative is to buy bottled water and use it as your soft water starting point—a good way to go broke through water changes. By now you are beginning to understand why I recommend matching the fish to your water, rather than the other way around! In any case, we don't really have to worry about providing soft water for our Central American cichlids, as they are all capable of adapting to hard water, and most inhabit areas where the water is hard.

# Small Central American Cichlids

We're going to cover the individual species in groups based on size, beginning with the smallest ones. That doesn't mean that only small cichlids should be kept together. Some of the small ones are so aggressive that they dominate some of the larger ones. I will try to make special notice of the small species that can be mixed with big cichlids. I should mention that none of this is absolute. Some strange combinations have been made under unusual circumstances. Just one example was when a friend ended up with a quite good-looking tank of a nearly 2-foot-long (60 cm) *Cichlasoma (Nandopsis) dovii* and several colonies of *Neetroplus nematopus*. The *N. nematopus* were placed in as food for the *C. dovii,* but not all of them got eaten in the huge tank. Several reached spawning size and set up housekeeping. The *C. dovii* was never harassed, of course, and he never bothered them, as he had apparently gotten used to them as tankmates.

That, of course, is an example of a combination that would not be recommended, but certain ones can be. As just one example, the small *Neetroplus nematopus* can be combined with the fairly large *Cichlasoma (Herichthys) nicaraguense.*

But let us get on with our "small fry," which, of course, are classified as such only in the cichlid realm. I am providing the popular name when one is available. Usually the reason there is a popular name is because the fish is sufficiently popular that the name has taken hold or the species in question has been in the hobby for a sufficient length of time that a common name has become recognized. With such fishes, oddly enough, some of the popular names are actually obsolete scientific names.

Please keep in mind that the names in parentheses are the scientific names that most likely will end up as names with full

*Aequidens coeruleopunctatus*, **an adult male.**

generic status. Most of these names are the "sections" that Regan suggested for breaking up the Central American species of *Cichlasoma*. These divisions seem to have been based on feeding methods and the structures that evolved to facilitate them. Some of the names are relatively new ones that modern ichthyologists have erected, but they may not yet be accepted by all ichthyologists, who tend to be conservative as a group anyway about name changes.

There are well over a hundred Central American cichlid species, but space limitations prevent covering all of them here. Some that I have left out are those that other cichlidophiles greatly treasure. For that I apologize. Obviously, personal preference plays a role here.

### Aequidens coeruleopunctatus

Although this species has no popular name and is not especially colorful, I consider it to be worth keeping as the only representative of its genus in Central America. It is found from Costa Rica to Panama. Although a good parent, it is relatively peaceful, much like the species in the *Thorichthys* group. The males don't quite reach 6 inches (15 cm) in length.

### Cichlasoma (Archocentrus) nigrofasciatum

This fish has often been called the "missionary cichlid," as it so often entices a neophyte into the cichlid hobby. It is not beautiful, but it is unerringly a good parent, and on the very first try, too! Further, it spawns at a young age, and it seems to be in the process of either spawning or raising young during most of its life span. A further favorable attribute of convict cichlids is that they

The female is the upper fish in this pair of convict cichlids, *Cichlasoma nigrofasciatum.* These fish show the color of wild-caught specimens, with the female having a reddish cast to the belly area; in females from other areas within the convict cichlid's range the cast could be yellowish instead.

spawn at a very small size, with the male barely over an inch (2.5 cm) long and the female reaching barely an inch in size.

Convicts cichlids are quite common, but they never lose their appeal. A recent innovation among cichlidophiles is to try to collect all the color varieties of this species. Since it is spread over a wide area of Central America, there is considerable variation in coloration, depending upon the location where the species is found. There are especially red color forms that are found in Honduras. In these specimens, the red is found on both male and female. On the female, it covers more of the body, producing a flaming belly region and red all the way up to the dorsal fin. In the more common types, the male shows no red, but the female sports a copper coloration in the ventral (belly) region.

Convict cichlids are known as fierce protectors of their young. For example, a famous story involves a surplus of convicts that were being fed to a piranha in a Los Angeles fish shop. Some of the babies escaped and matured to spawning size. The resulting pair nearly chased the piranha out of its own tank, even though it looked like a whale as compared to the cichlids, and the shop owner had to move the piranha for its own safety.

The *Archocentrus* group is one that feeds on the bottom, picking up foods

A female white convict cichlid; white convict cichlids show varying degrees of coverage by colors ranging from shades of yellow to shades of orange.

Fiercely protective of its free-swimming fry, this parent convict cichlid has no hesitation about attacking its owner's intruding hand.

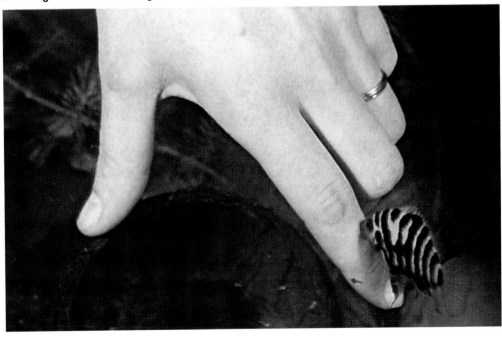

*Cichlasoma sajica.*

opportunistically. The food can vary from invertebrates inhabiting the substrate to a mixture of organic matter that ichthyologists euphemistically call "grut." The parents feed the young off a specialized body slime that is secreted by both parents. This supplying a supplementary "milk" is very common among Central American cichlids. The parents also supply food for the young by chewing up food that is too large for them and spitting it out in the school of young. They also "sweep" the bottom with their anal fins to stir up any possible food for the young. All these behaviors, though typical of many cichlids, are what have endeared this particular species to aquarists around the world.

### Cichlasoma (Archocentrus) sajica

There is no popular name for this cichlid, as it was described only recently, and it is very likely the smallest of our Central American cichlids. The species name *sajica* is the Spanish rendition of an Indian name, so it is pronounced "saw-HEE-ka." Although not particularly colorful, it has interesting markings. It has nearly all the behaviors of the convict cichlid, and it changes colors when spawning. (Convicts merely darken slightly.)

### Cichlasoma (Archocentrus) septemfasciatum
### Copper Cichlid

This is another cichlid that changes dramatically when spawning. The popular name comes from the copper-like coloring that often covers the body of the female. Something that all of the *Archocentrus* group share is that the female is pretty much in charge of the eggs before they hatch, while the male guards the perimeter. Once the eggs hatch, the male aids in moving the young to a hole that has been dug. As a matter of fact, several holes are dug while the young are becoming free-swimming. The period of time involved is about four days, and the reason for moving the young from one hole to another has been debated. One early theory was that it made a moving target of the young, as they didn't stay at a permanent address. Although that may be part of the reason for the behavior, there is overwhelming pressure to keep the young clean. As they are transferred via mouth by the parents from hole to hole, they get cleansed of debris and any bacteria or fungus that may be attacking them or growing as a culture in the debris.

Through a sorting error, this species was originally introduced into this country as *Cichlasoma spilurum,* and it is found in the older aquarium literature under that name. When this species spawns, the female develops a dark mask that looks very much like a knight with his visor pulled down, ready for battle. While not a knight, a guarding copper female is truly ready for battle!

### Cichlasoma (Archocentrus) spilurum

Although superficially similar in color to the convict cichlid, *C. spilurum* has stripes of a different pattern, and the males often have a yellow coloration to the body. An interesting point among the very similar *Archocentrus* listed here is that the farther away they get from each other's range, the more they resemble one another, with the individuals living sympatrically with other species showing the most difference in coloration. Biologically this makes sense, as hybridization from a failure to recognize the different species would spell the end of the line for the genetic material of the species involved, as hybrids seldom prosper or reproduce successfully in the wild.

This *Cichlasoma septemfasciatum* is showing a good amount of the coloring that gave the species its common name of copper cichlid.

*Cichlasoma spilurum.* **Note the blue eye, the reason this fish is sometimes called the blue-eyed cichlid.**

### *Cichlasoma (Thorichthys) aureum*
### Golden Cichlid

Actually, there are several popular names for color variations of this quite charming cichlid, including "gold flash." The most popular of this group in the aquarium trade is the firemouth cichlid, *Cichlasoma (Thorichthys) meeki,* and all of the *Thorichthys* group greatly resemble one another. They are substrate sifters, but they don't run the gravel out through the gills, as is so typical of *Geophagus.* Instead, they turn the sand over in the mouth and then spit it out. In the wild, they feed primarily on invertebrates that they find in the sand, mostly insect larvae. In the aquarium, they take food opportunistically, and they are good eaters and hardy aquarium fishes.

The species from this group really push the small cichlid category, as in several species the male reaches a length of 6 inches (15 cm), with the female about 5 inches (12.5 cm). But golden cichlids are quite mild as compared to cichlids in general. True enough, they are fierce protectors of their young, but they are less capable than many other cichlids of inflicting damage, and when not spawning

*Cichlasoma aureum.*

THE GUIDE TO OWNING CENTRAL AMERICAN CICHLIDS

*Cichlasoma ellioti,* a look-alike of the firemouth cichlid, a much more commonly available fish. Shown is an adult female.

they are relatively quiescent. I have kept them with angels, for example, something that could not be done with the cichlids in the next chapter, with the possible exception of one or two species.

There are two main color variations of this species, with one being known as the "blue flash," sporting primarily blue coloration, and the other the "gold flash," showing more reds and golds. The fact is that some red (or gold) and blue is shown in each variation, but the division is understandable once you become familiar with this species.

There has been a renewed interest in *C. aureus* because of recent new imports and because of the fact that it is relatively new to the hobby. The *Thorichthys* division is popular enough that some cichlid fans tend to specialize in just this group.

### *Cichlasoma (Thorichthys) ellioti*

Although there is no popular name for this species, it has become particularly popular with cichlid specialists in recent years, for the same reasons given above with *C. aureus.* This species is found in eastern Mexico.

One of the interesting aspects of the *Thorichthys* group is that the male and female share duties in the care of the young. That is, the male takes his turn at fanning the eggs while the female guards the perimeter or feeds briefly. Another trait of interest is the spot on the operculum (the gill cover). This apparently is an eye spot that is used in frontal displays. That

Male firemouth cichlid, *Cichlasoma meeki*, standing by while his spawning partner is depositing eggs.

means that the spots are enlarged when the fish confronts another fish of the same or different species. The gill covers and a membrane below the neck flare out, much like the ruff on a gamecock, and make the fish look larger. This is a threatening display, and it has the advantage of providing the threatener with two extra eyes, both of them large. This jibes well with information ethologists (those who study animal behavior) have gathered that animals seem to be innately afraid of eyes, and the bigger the eyes are, the more frightening they are. (Just think of people and horror movies, with large eyes glowing in the dark.)

In any case, with this group of fishes, the displays help drive off other fish species without actual aggression. That may be one reason that this group is of a somewhat milder temperament.

### Cichlasoma (Thorichthys) meeki
### Firemouth Cichlid

This species has long been a favorite in the aquarium, even though it is not suitable for the typical community aquarium. The reasons for its popularity are obvious. It has a distinctive shape, and its coloration is quite pleasing also. It has always been one of my favorites. The firemouth cichlid can be kept in a community aquarium until spawning time arises. Then the other fishes are driven off mercilessly. Firemouths spawn when the male is a mere 3 inches (7.5 cm), with the female being about 2.5 inches (6.3 cm) in length. However, the male can eventually reach nearly 6 inches (15 cm) in length. As compared to many other cichlids, the pairs seem to stay together well in the home aquarium, with no spats in between spawning.

The firemouth's bluff may be even more impressive than those of the other fishes in this group. That is, its frontal threatening display may be more effective. That is because of the red coloration that is more intense in this species, especially toward

The female of this pair of rainbow cichlids, *Herotilapia multispinosa*, continues to lay eggs on the already egg-covered flat rock as the male hovers above, awaiting his opportunity to fertilize them.

the front. For some reason, red coloration also is intimidating to fishes, a fact discovered by ethologists.

There are color differences in this species too, depending upon the fish's place of origin. The species ranges from southern Mexico to Guatemala, being found primarily on the Yucatan peninsula. Some species have more blue spangles, and with others there is more emphasis on the red. And it should be mentioned that there is some variation in the coloration in a single population of this species in one locality, with some specimens showing a brighter red than others. The most beautiful, and therefore the most popular, specimens are those that show a balance of bright red with lots of blue spangles.

### Herotilapia multispinosa
### Rainbow Cichlid

This fish is a candidate for the title of being the smallest of the Central American cichlids, with the males reaching only 3 inches (7.5 cm), or only a little more. This is another species that seems capable of defending its young without committing total mayhem on its tankmates. This fish is distinctive from other Central American cichlids in that it has tricuspid (three-pointed) teeth. These teeth enable it to more easily harvest filamentous algae, which make up a good portion of its diet. In the aquarium it will take all foods, but some vegetable matter should be a part of its diet, even if it is only dry foods designed for herbivores.

### Neetroplus nematopus
### Poor Man's Tropheus

This species is somewhat analogous to the *Tropheus* of Lake Tanganyika in that it lives off the algae that grow on rocks in the lakes and rivers in which it is found. It somewhat resembles *Tropheus* in shape, too, and this fact has resulted in its being dubbed with the popular name "poor man's *Tropheus.*" This makes devotees of the

*Neetroplus nematopus* in non-breeding coloration.

*Neetroplus nematopus* in breeding color. Notice that in addition to the darkening of the body, the mid-body vertical bar has turned from black to white.

species—and of Central American cichlids in general—bristle, for they feel that *N. nematopus* is more than the equal of any *Tropheus*, most especially in behavior.

To be fair, many *Tropheus* are more colorful, and they will probably always be highly priced because of their small spawns. In addition, *Tropheus* can be difficult to spawn in captivity. In the case of *Neetroplus* it is just the opposite. Just try to stop these guys from spawning! They run the convict cichlid a close second on propensity to spawn and efficiency in protecting their young. This fish is found from Costa Rica to Nicaragua in lakes and rivers, including Lakes Managua and Nicaragua.

An interesting aspect to this fish is its reversal of colors at spawning time. The dark stripe down the side becomes quite white, and the body becomes nearly jet black. So in spawning colors *N. nematopus*

really does resemble *Tropheus duboisi* adults.

## COMMENTS

For those who are just beginning with Central American cichlids and want to set up a community tank of cichlids, I would suggest convict cichlids, firemouths, rainbows, and *Neetroplus nematopus*. The convicts will probably spawn first and then the *Neetroplus*. Be sure to put in plenty of rocks. Things will get the roughest when the young become free swimming. It is possible to siphon the young out at that time and raise them in a separate tank. But it is difficult for many cichlidophiles to do that to the parents, and if you leave even one baby in the tank, the parents will still harass the other fish. The fry of all of these cichlids can be raised on a combination of finely powdered food and either live or frozen newly hatched brine shrimp.

# Medium-Size Central American Cichlids

Of course, I should once again caution that we are speaking in relative terms, for some of these medium cichlids will be quite large, most of them eventually reaching over 6 inches (15 cm), especially the males. Cichlids are generally among the largest of the freshwater fauna, but they are not the biggest. Many of the aquarium catfishes and a few fishes of other families get larger. In Central America, however, cichlids make up the bulk of the larger freshwater fishes. So "medium" to us may seem quite large to most other tropical fish hobbyists.

Even so, many of these cichlids are quite gentle. As just one example, *Cichlasoma (Hypsophrys) nicaraguense* could be combined with firemouths, as it is a mild fish even though it reaches a good 10 inches (25 cm) in length. Others have evolved very truculent temper-aments in order to protect their young. I well recall a female *Cichlasoma (Nandopsis) urophthalmus*

actually lunging out of the water at my hand as I was trying to shade the water in order to view her with her young in her home waters in Yucatan. Pairs of such species may be difficult to keep together unless the tank is of a sufficiently large size. If the tank is not big enough, horrific fights may erupt. Since the female is considerably smaller than the male, she gets the worst of it and may be killed. Prudent cichlid hobbyists with insufficiently large tanks use a glass barrier between the two and have it propped up about a 1/4 inch to allow the male to fertilize the eggs. The fry can then be left in with the parents, as the cichlids, versatile critters that they are, manage to act as though the entire thing is a normal spawning event.

A lot of these medium-size cichlids really are more than just passingly attractive, although "handsome" might be a better term for such robust animals.

A nicely (if you like thick lips) thick-lipped red devil, *Cichlasoma labiatum.*

### *Cichlasoma (Amphilophus) labiatum*
### Red Devil

When these cichlids were first imported, dealers were almost tempted to put them in ocean water, as they resembled the Garibaldi, a large California damselfish, in color. Exporters had actually mixed up red devils with red Midas cichlids, *Cichlasoma (Amphilophus) citrinellum.* For that reason, the Midas cichlid is still called a red devil in some circles, but it tends to be golden rather than red, and it has a less pointed snout. The large lips of the red devil tend to regress under captive conditions for some reason that is not completely understood. These cichlids were not named red devils without reason, as they are very aggressive and have the dentition to back it up. Nothing could seemingly be kept with them, but it was later discovered that they could be kept (in very large tanks, of course) with a number of other cichlids— any of the tough ones, that is—while growing up.

With all of these cichlids, the best way to breed them is to get about six of the juveniles and allow them to pair up naturally. Of course, once a pair spawns, you will have to remove the others unless you have a 2000-gallon (7600-liter) tank! The juveniles are gray in coloration and then turn speckled before they turn red. Interestingly enough, the red coloration is quite variable, and it is often fringed with black (the most beautiful pattern, in my

An example of the red variety of the Midas cichlid, *Cichlasoma citrinellum*, often confused with the red devil—but note the thinner lips and more rounded snout.

This particular *Cichlasoma rostratum* could equal the spangling on a Jack Dempsey at its showiest best.

opinion), and a fascinating tidbit is that in the wild many of the individual specimens stay gray. This fact has been much studied by scientists.

The male can reach nearly a foot (30 cm) in length, but it takes about three years to attain such a size. The pairs will spawn when only 6 inches (15 cm) long.

### Cichlasoma (Amphilophus) rostratum

Now for something a little easier-going. This species is more somber in coloration, but it has a lot of attractive blue spangles, and it is considerably less aggressive than *C. labiatum*. In addition, it reaches a length of only 6 to 7 inches (15-17.5 cm).

The distribution of this fish is on the Atlantic slope from Costa Rica to Nicaragua. This is one of the medium-size species that can be kept with the smaller ones.

### Cichlasoma (Amphilophus) octofasciatum
### Jack Dempsey

You can tell by the popular name of this fish how long it has been in the hobby, as Jack Dempsey became heavyweight boxing champion of the world back in 1919. Most people these days simply refer to the fish as "Dempseys." And the fact is that although Dempseys are less aptly named now that much more combative cichlids have been introduced to the market (they're not nearly so aggressive as the red devil and some others, for example), they were comparatively very rough customers during the years when they first became popular, and the species is durable and tough enough to be kept with such fish in a tank that is reasonably large. It is found on the Atlantic slope, from Mexico to Belize.

An adult male Jack Dempsey, *Cichlasoma octofasciatum,* in fine condition.

Juveniles look primarily black, without the blue spangling that really "makes" the appearance of this fish. It takes patience to see this fish at its best, as it takes slightly over a year to fully mature. Yet I have known of small specimens, barely 3 inches long, breeding in captivity. How rare this is would be difficult to say, but it most assuredly is non-existent in the wild.

Like all other Central American cichlids, the Jack Dempsey prefers slightly hard and alkaline water, and also like the others, it is quite adaptable. It is a long-time favorite and deservedly so.

Incidentally, this species can be squeezed into the subgenus *Amphilophus* only with a shoehorn. It is something of a stretch to put it there, and ichthyologists may eventually place it in a genus of its own, as it doesn't fit clearly into any of the proposed genera or subgenera. The males reach a length of about 8 inches (20 cm).

### *Cichlasoma (Hypsophrys) nicaraguense*
### Parrot Cichlid

Although males can reach a length of 10 inches, this is a rather gentle cichlid as compared to the others. Certainly it is in the running for the title of most beautiful of the Central American cichlids. The females are actually more colorful than the males, but the males are certainly not somber in coloration. They simply have fewer gold and more emerald colors.

The species is found in Lakes Managua and Nicaragua as well as in numerous other lakes and rivers down to Costa Rica. The parrot cichlid's behavior is distinct in many ways. For one thing, it inhabits the sandy

The parrot cichlid, *Cichlasoma nicaraguense*, beautifully even if not gaudily colored.

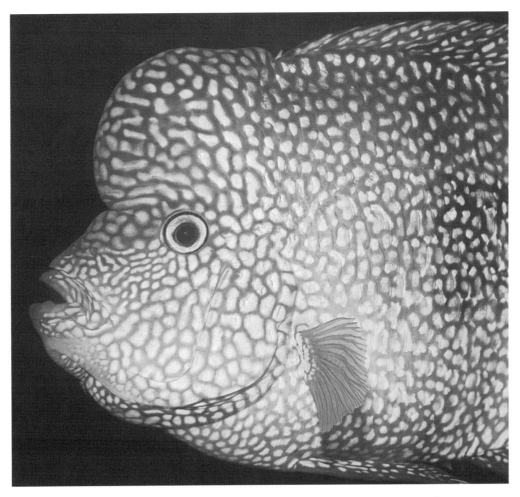

Closeup of the head area of a fully adult (aged, in fact) male *Cichlasoma carpinte,* the green Texas cichlid, previously confused with the real (really from Texas, that is) Texas cichlid.

areas of lakes and rivers, and the pairs spawn in a sandy pit, producing bright golden eggs. These eggs are non-adhesive and actually bounce around to some extent when the female fans them. Additionally, groups of females form a territory, into which no predators are permitted to enter, that serves as a communal nursery for the young. Such behavior is not often seen, even among cichlids!

This is one of those larger species that can easily be kept with the smaller cichlids, and it should not be kept with some of the tougher ones, such as red devils and Texas cichlids.

### *Cichlasoma (Herichthys) carpinte*
### Green Texas Cichlid

The popular name of this species came about from the confusion of this species with the Texas cichlid, *Cichlasoma (Herichthys) cyanoguttatum.* This species is found in northeastern Mexico on the Atlantic slope; its range does not extend up into the United States, as does the range of the Texas cichlid. The males reach a length of slightly over 6 inches (15 cm).

*Cichlasoma carpinte*, full side view.

### *Cichlasoma (Herichthys) cyanoguttatum* Texas Cichlid

Truth to tell, the Texas cichlid has many popular names. In the aquarium hobby, it has been known as the Texas cichlid and the pearl cichlid. The first name was given because the fish's range extends from Mexico north into Texas, making it the only cichlid native to the US, and the second was given because of the color of the front part of the fish when it is in spawning coloration. But popular names among anglers have ranged from "Rio Grande perch" to *mojarra* (in Mexico). Such variation in popular names helps illustrate one of the advantages of scientific names.

The Texas cichlid is durable and tough enough to be kept with the red devil.

Males reach a length of 7 to 8 inches (17.5 to 20 cm).

### *Cichlasoma (Herichthys) labridens*

This fish from northeastern Mexico on the Atlantic slope is kept primarily by specialists who are willing to keep the more obscure Central American cichlids. Surprisingly, while Americans were going crazy over African cichlids, the crack German aquarists were in the process of accumulating the Central American cichlids, and this species was one that excited them, mostly because they had imported some red "morphs" that were not typical of the species. Even so, the species has a following because of its interesting behavior and golden coloration.

Males attain a length of 6 to 7 inches (15 to 17.5 cm).

THE GUIDE TO OWNING CENTRAL AMERICAN CICHLIDS

Texas cichlid, *Cichlasoma cyanoguttatum.*

### *Cichlasoma (Nandopsis) salvini*
### Tricolor Cichlid

This is a beautiful but very aggressive cichlid from the Atlantic slope of Mexico to Guatemala, where it is quite common in Lake Peten. This is another one of those cichlids in which the female is more colorful than the male, but both of them can look quite lovely. These fish are predators upon large invertebrates and small fishes, including the fry of other cichlid species. This species will mix well with Dempseys, and they can also be kept with red devils. Of course, all bets are off when spawning time arrives, as whichever species has the fry is likely to dominate.

Males reach a size of about 8 inches (20 cm), but the fish spawn at a much smaller size.

### *Cichlasoma (Nandopsis) tetracanthus*
### Cuban Cichlid

The Cuban cichlid has been in the hobby for quite some time. I should rephrase that. It was early in the hobby and then disappeared until some

*Cichlasoma labridens.*

The female *Cichlasoma salvini* can be even more colorful than the male, but regardless of their sex individuals of this species are rough customers.

enterprising collectors got a batch of them from Cuba to dispense to cichlid breeders. Although not an extremely colorful fish, it has attractive coloration, and the fish are hearty aquarium inhabitants with voracious appetites.

The males reach about 8 inches (20 cm) in length. These are fairly aggressive fish, but they can be kept with Dempseys, red devils, and tricolor cichlids.

### Cichlasoma (Nandopsis) urophthalmus Orange Tiger

I couldn't resist including this fish, if only because of the female that leaped at my hand in Yucatan when I threatened her young. I have had many cichlids, including red devils, bite my hand to bleeding when I put it into their tank, especially when they were tending young. But I had never had one leap out of the water at it before. Found on the Atlantic slope of Central America, this very adaptable fish also inhabits the mangroves of the ocean! In fact, it has been seen competing in the rocky areas of Isla Mujeres, an island off the Yucatan peninsula. The fish work the roots of the mangroves in search of small fishes and large invertebrates. Obviously they are good feeders, but they are also among the most aggressive cichlids, so plan accordingly and keep them with fishes

*Cichlasoma tetracanthus.*

*Cichlasoma urophthalmus*—not the best-looking cichlid around, but hard to match for ferocity in defense of its fry.

*Geophagus crassilabris,* a mouthbrooding species that is relatively much milder in temperament than most of the other Central American cichlids.

having similar levels of aggression (the red devils again!).

The males can easily reach 9 inches (22.5 cm) in length.

### Geophagus crassilabris

Naturally, I had to include the only *Geophagus* species that occurs in Central America. These animals are distinctive in shape and sport a nice bronze coloration with turquoise highlights. Gentle enough that they could be kept with *C. nicaraguense* and all the small cichlids we listed in the last chapter, they come from Panama.

The males reach a length of about 9 inches (22.5 cm).

# Big and Bad

Actually, one or two of the fish species that I list here will be less aggressive than some of the small ones. But generally speaking these guys are pretty rough. And since they get to be as large as they do, often the only way to spawn them is to utilize a divider in the tank, either a glass raised 1/4 inch or a grating made from a plastic fluorescent lighting diffuser. People who keep these fish, and I (blush!) have

"Oh, what big teeth you have, Grandma," said Little Red Riding Hood as she peered interestedly into her tank of wolf cichlids before going out to feed her pit bull terriers.

*Cichlasoma friedrichsthalii*, the smallest and least homicidal of the guapotes.

done so myself, claim that they are worth the trouble because of their interesting behavior and, in some cases, beautiful coloration. I mean, if you have a 200-gallon tank (760 liters), what difference does it make whether you have hundreds of tiny fish or one or two really big ones? Well, a lot, actually, as the large fish impact the water more than a hundred small ones, so you will be making lots of partial water changes!

A common way to keep these fish is to keep just one as a kind of pet. They are such intelligent fishes that they react with their keepers, much like a dog or a cat. Hobbyists even provide toys, such as floating Ping-Pong balls, and that is not a bad idea. If you are not around a lot, just one fish in a tank by itself can suffer a certain amount from sensory deprivation. Providing various items of interest that the fish can investigate is one way of circumventing the problem of a boring

tank for a single fish. Even though the fish is kept by itself, it should have rocks and tunnels with which it can indulge itself. In any case, keeping one of these monsters solo in the tank is one viable option.

### *Cichlasoma (Nandopsis) dovii*
### Wolf Cichlid

Here is a cichlid that is a candidate for the "baddest of the bad"! This fish predator has such powerful jaws that if a fish is too big to swallow, it consumes it by ripping it to pieces. Rarely is it possible to keep one of these individuals with another fish, even a large armored catfish, as it simply won't tolerate another individual within the confines of the aquarium space that most of us are able to provide. Yet individuals of this species were kept as pets and were the all-time favorites of two famous aquarists. One was the late Gene Wolfsheimer, a real pioneer in the tropical fish hobby, and the other was Guy Jordan, a co-founder of the American Cichlid Association. Gene's

*Cichlasoma managuense*—not for the faint-hearted and not for a 10-gallon tank.

individual was a red-colored variant (there is a blue form, too, but both the red and blue forms are rare), and she was the showpiece of his large hatchery. He had two heavy pieces of cover glass on her tank, as she would knock a single cover off when she wanted attention! The pictures of this magnificent animal graced the pages of aquarium magazines a quarter of a century ago, as she was the only *C. dovii* in the country at the time.

Anyway, you get the idea: *C. dovii* individuals are about as rough and tough as they come and are extremely intelligent. They have been bred in captivity a number of times. Usually this involves separating the parents with some sort of partition. In the wild, the parents cooperate wonderfully in order to protect the young. Males reach nearly 2 feet in length, but these animals are definite candidates for the most intelligent of all cichlids—and

surely that includes all other fishes, too!

### *Cichlasoma (Nandopsis) friedrichsthalii*

This is a small version of the wolf cichlid, reaching "only" 10 inches (25 cm) in length. It is found on the Atlantic slope from Mexico to Belize. An appealing yellow variety of this species is found in Lake Peten in Guatemala. Surprisingly, the regular and drabber specimens are the ones that most hobbyists are keeping.

In addition to being smaller, members of this species are somewhat tamer in behavior than wolf cichlids. In truth, it is difficult to make generalizations about the three "guapotes" (as they are called in Central America). That would include *C. dovii*, *C. friedrichsthalii*, and *C. managuense*.

### *Cichlasoma (Nandopsis) managuense*
### Jaguar Cichlid

This species is found on the Atlantic slope from Costa Rica to Honduras, and it is mid-way in size between *C. friedrichsthalii* and the wolf cichlid. It can be a nice compromise, as individuals of this species can be quite fiery. A humorous situation is that many fish kept as individuals will be downright friendly with their owners but totally pugnacious with strangers. I remember an occasion when my wife was entranced with the beauty and grace of a specimen at a friend's house. When she leaned down to look at it more closely, the fish hit the glass so hard and with such fury that it actually scared her! Not all specimens are so hostile. One of the interesting features about such intelligent fishes is that there is a lot of individual variation among the different specimens. Some individuals will even be slightly shy, but I admit that that is rare. I well recall one specimen kept alone that had apparently appropriated the bulletin board and the birdcage (each at opposite ends of the tank) as his possessions. As long as you did not approach or touch the bulletin board or birdcage, you were safe from having the fish hit the glass to rail at you.

Obviously these fish are quite intelligent. It would be difficult to determine with certainty whether they are any less smart than *C. dovii*, but the general opinion among cichlidophiles favors the latter. The males reach a length of about eleven inches.

### Cichlasoma (Nandopsis) trimaculatum
### Trimac

This red-eyed cichlid practically breathes fire. When James Langhammer was curator

*Cichlasoma trimaculatum.* **The red eyes might be a tip-off to the temperament of this species.**

*Cichlasoma umbriferum.* **The basketmouth cichlid can turn other fishes into basket cases.**

of the Detroit Zoo, he wrote of the trimacs that took feeder mice away from the alligators! He also related how guarding females would leap out of the water at threatening hands. This is another species that delights people who like rough fish. They are found on the Pacific slope of Mexico.

These cichlids are good parents, and the best way to get a pair is to obtain about six to eight young and raise them up and let them pair off naturally. The males reach a length of about 14 inches (35 cm).

### *Cichlasoma (Nandopsis) umbriferum*
### Basketmouth Cichlid

This is a Central American cichlid whose

Male *Cichlasoma maculicauda* **showing off his black belt.**

THE GUIDE TO OWNING CENTRAL AMERICAN CICHLIDS

range extends down into South America to Colombia on the Atlantic slope and reaches north to Panama. This beautiful blue cichlid competes with *C. dovii* as the largest Central American cichlid. It inhabits open water and preys upon schools of livebearers and the very common *Astyanax* that inhabit that area.

Although dramatic in display, the basketmouth cichlid seems less aggressive than *C. dovii*. When they first appeared nearly 20 years ago, it was predicted that they would replace *C. dovii* as the pet for advanced hobbyists, but it never quite happened. Just not ornery enough, I guess. But they are quite popular for such large fish. The males attain nearly 2 feet (60 cm) in length, but they are deeper-bodied than the wolf cichlid. And, lest I leave the impression that these fish are non-aggressive, I should correct that. They may not be hitting the glass all the time the way *C. dovii* specimens do, but they are plenty aggressive—and they have the size and dentition to back up their combativeness.

### *Cichlasoma (Theraps) maculicauda*
### Black Belt Cichlid

At last we get to the gentle giants of the cichlid world. This is the most widely distributed cichlid in Central America, inhabiting coastal lagoons and estuaries as well as lakes and rivers. Black belts are colorful fish, and the parents can be kept together normally without any problems. As with many other cichlids, the best way to pair them up is to raise up about six young and let them pair up naturally as they mature.

The male reaches a length of little over a foot (30 cm); however, these fish have such deep bodies that we have to be careful not to underestimate their true size.

### *Cichlasoma (Theraps) argentea*

Here is a species that is not only gentle but also is somewhat fragile as contrasted against those cichlids that "you couldn't kill with a hammer," as an old friend would say. It has a delicate coloration, a lacy appearance that must be seen in the flesh to be appreciated. Certainly it is appreciated, as specimens of this species have won best in show awards at at least one big cichlid convention.

Males reach just over a foot (30 cm) in length, but like *C. maculicauda* this is a deep-bodied species.

## COMMENTS

Obviously, I have been unable to include all the desirable large Central American cichlids. Personal taste has been a factor, but truth to tell I have excluded some of my favorites, too. The purpose here was to provide an overview of some of the marvelous large cichlids that are available.

*Cichlasoma argentea*, **male.**

# Breeding Central American Cichlids

In many ways, breeding Central American cichlids is a snap. For the simple truth of the matter is that cichlids breed themselves. All they need is decent water, a decent diet, and other cichlids of the same species. There is the rub! Trying to get grown cichlids to pair up can be a problem. It is easier with the smaller species, as they can maneuver and hide better in the tank. The time-tested method has been to avoid problems involved with trying to pair up adults by obtaining about six juveniles and allowing them to grow up and pair off naturally.

Many hobbyists utilize a special breeding tank, but it is perfectly feasible to allow the pair to spawn in a community tank of cichlids. Simply remove the fry by siphoning some of them out once they are free swimming. They can then be put into a smaller tank in which they can be raised free from the predation of the other adult fish in the tank. Naturally, the water should be of the same quality and temperature as that of the community tank.

The other option is to place a pair or an aggregate of a single species in a breeding tank. The main advantages here are that you can use a smaller tank and there are fewer potential predators on the fry. The parents won't eat the young, of course, but the other individuals of the same species may have no compunctions about such cannibalism. A further advantage to a breeding tank is that it can be set up in a manner to facilitate breeding or protect the female.

To understand what you need to do it is necessary to understand how cichlids spawn in nature. With Central American cichlids, there are many variations on a theme, but nearly all of them spawn in pairs. In the wild, these animals pair up. There is an elaborate courtship pattern. Not all the cichlids spawn. Only those

A pair of white convict cichlids in pre-spawning maneuvers directly above a flat rock on which the eggs were later deposited. The smaller but more colorful female has begun to respond to the advances of the male, but her ovipositor has not yet descended. In other cases of Central American cichlid matings, the genital papillae of both male and female fish of the pair can be visible well before actual spawning begins.

most fit are able to find mates and successfully raise the young. Evolution has shaped the species so that each individual fish favors certain characteristics in the other sex. We can identify with this as humans, for we all know what a good-looking girl or guy is, but there are other factors that enter into things. Girls tend to prefer tall males, and males that have a good personality and have certain accomplishments to their credit are preferred, too. Similarly, Central American cichlid females tend to prefer larger males with an appearance that exemplifies the species—just as in humans! Also, the female cichlids tend to find males that have acquired a territory to be irresistible. This trait varies, to some degree, from species to species. The elaborate courtship, which may last for days or even weeks, is not well understood by the scientists who study these fishes, but one reason for it is that it is believed to give the fish practice at functioning as pairs, something that will stand them in good stead when the time comes for them to defend their eggs against other predacious fish.

When the bond is finally established, the pair begins cleaning off a rock or a submerged tree branch that will eventually be the spot where they will deposit the adhesive eggs. (There are exceptions in this regard. For example,

Female *Cichlasoma septemfasciatus* standing guard over eggs she has laid on the inside surface of an upright piece of coconut shell. Most Central American cichlids choose a relatively flat solid horizontal surface on which to lay their eggs, but chosen sites also may be inclined at an angle, and sometimes the eggs are laid while the female is upside down.

THE GUIDE TO OWNING CENTRAL AMERICAN CICHLIDS

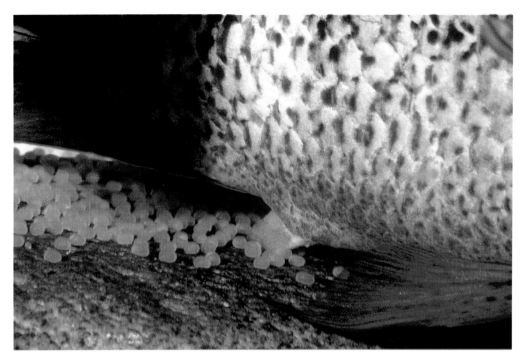

An *Herichthys* species female in the process of extruding an egg from her ovipositor to join the rest of the clutch she has already put down.

Here the male of a pair of firemouths is fertilizing the eggs deposited on the wall of a flowerpot that has had its bottom removed.

The female of a pair of green Texas cichlids is using her pectoral fins to fan the fertilized eggs on the rock below her.

*Cichlasoma nicaraguense* lays non-adhesive eggs in river sand, often even tunneling into the banks, creating a cave in which non-adhesive eggs will be laid.) While cleaning off the rock, the pair begins to become quite territorial. That is, they will exclude other fish from the territory they have claimed as the site for their eggs. Many species, but certainly not all, show a definite color change during this time, spouting special spawning colors. Some species simply brighten in their normal coloration, but others show special striping or dark masks. An example of extreme color change is *Neetroplus nematopus*. In this species, the body colors are reversed. A dark vertical stripe changes from black to white, and the body changes from a light olive coloration to dark, nearly black.

When spawning time finally arrives, the male stands guard while the female deposits her eggs. Then he glides over the eggs, carefully depositing his sperm on each one. In a variation of this, the male glides along right behind the female, fertilizing the eggs as she lays them. When the eggs are finally laid and fertilized, the female usually guards and fans them while the male guards the perimeters of the territory. This is not always the case. In some species, male and female spell each other in the task of fanning the eggs and guarding the outer perimeters. Although the pair will feed during this time, the eggs and fry take priority. Feeding is only a secondary concern. There are two reasons for fanning the eggs. Firstly, the fanning passes new water over the eggs, so the exchange of gases is facilitated. (As the eggs develop, the embryos begin to respire, so they need oxygen, and they need to get rid of carbon dioxide.) The other function of the fanning is to keep the eggs free of debris that might foster pathogenic organisms. If an egg does die from bacteria or fungus, the parent removes it so that it won't contaminate the others.

The eggs normally hatch in two to four days, depending on temperature and species, and the young are helpless "wigglers" when they first hatch out. They aren't able to swim, as a heavy yolk sac is still attached to the body, but they vibrate their tails vigorously, hence the term "wigglers." By the time the eggs hatch, the pair will have already dug a hole for them. During the time the wigglers are in the non-swimming stage, the pair will have dug several holes, and they transfer them periodically from one hole to another. Originally it was speculated that this behavior was for the purpose of keeping potential predators confounded as to the location of the fry. However, the primary advantage is now thought to be the cleaning that the fry get each time they

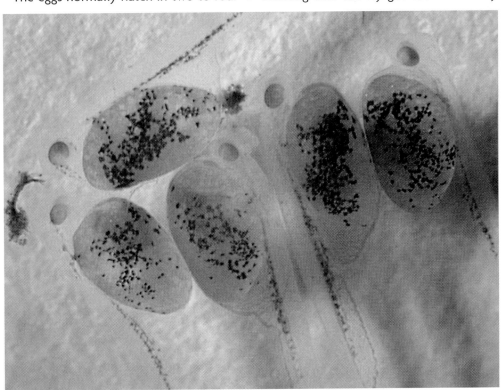

Recently hatched Midas cichlid fry. The babies' yolk sacs have begun to be used up, but the fry are still well within the wiggler stage.

are transferred by the parents. In fact, the parents mouth the fry quite a bit even when they are free swimming, so keeping them clean is apparently a prime consideration in keeping them healthy. Usually both parents begin to participate in the close care of the young once the fry have hatched, but this is not always true.

In nearly all Central American species, both parents begin to tend the young and cooperate in their defense when the fry become free swimming. It is at this time that the parents begin to herd the young. Now things change. Instead of the original territory, the area that the parents defend moves with them. The parents are especially vigilant and bellicose during this time. They innately seem to know which animals are dangerous to their young. For example, snails are viciously attacked and removed during the egg stage. But once the fry are free swimming, the gastropods are ignored.

I have observed cichlids with free-swimming young in Central America, and I have often been surprised at the large size to which the successful parents are able to tend their fry. In the wild, of course, the numbers of the fry drop off precipitously as they grow. The parents, while fighting one danger, are distracted by another, so the young suffer high losses from predation.

One of the most interesting things in the wild is to observe the cooperation of the parents in the defense of their young. They tend to stay at opposite ends of the school of fry and coordinate their positions relative to one another. But as perfect as their care is, it is not good enough to protect the entire brood. I have noticed in nature that the parents with the largest brood of good-sized young were those who were large enough and aggressive enough to commandeer spots in rocky areas that could be best described as miniature bays. I presumed that the advantage of such spots was that any potential predator would have to run a gantlet of other brood-caring cichlids.

Although cichlids are not dependent upon seasons for spawning, they do have special times of the year for spawning in the wild. An advantage of this behavior is to "swamp" predators so that they aren't able to subsist the entire year making a living off their young.

Another very interesting component of Central American parental care is that the parents provide a supplemental food for the young. Both parents secrete a specialized body slime that contains nutrients for the young. The fry feed only occasionally, and they do so by "glancing" off the bodies of the parents. This behavior was first noticed and reported upon by Professor George Barlow and his graduate students. The feeding behavior of the young of the South American cichlid discus is well known. But in that case the body slime of the parents is an obligatory first food, and the fry cling to the sides of the parents while feeding. In the case of the Central American cichlids, we have an intermediate step in that direction that seems to be simply a way of

*Cichlasoma sajica* showing the typically very dark coloring adopted by both spawning partners in this species. The free-swimming fry they are tending will from day to day become increasingly more adventurous and harder for the parents to control.

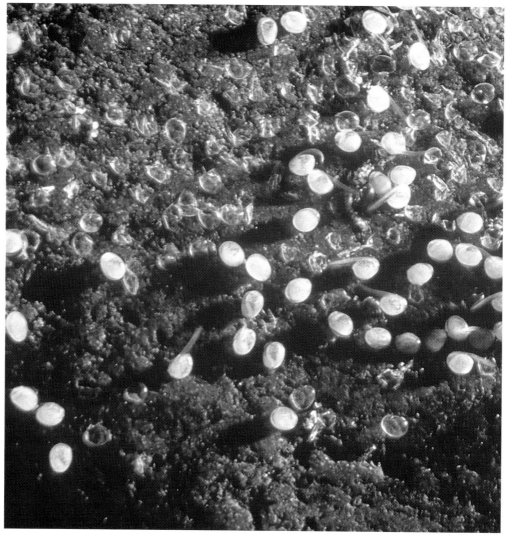

This view shows a little of everything in the results of a *Cichlasoma* spawning: newly hatched fry, the remains of hatched eggs, fertilized eggs, and unfertilized eggs.

providing the young with extra nutrition. It is an advantage but not an essential one. In the case of the discus, foods in the area are quite scarce for discus young. (And there may be other factors, too, that have caused the behavior to evolve.)

Once the fry have reached an age at which they have begun to disperse, the pair bond between the parents usually disappears and they depart from one another, probably never to meet again. So much for romance! But the demands of the environment don't give any advantage to having a pair stay together during their non-reproductive times—except in some species. With cichlids, there are always exceptions to the rule!

Now with all this information under our belts, we can get an idea of what we need to breed cichlids. Lots of rockwork in the aquarium is in order. The rocks will provide caves, hiding places, and places for the pair to deposit their eggs. An exception here is *Cichlasoma nicaraguense*, and the exception goes a long way toward demonstrating how versatile cichlids are. I got these cichlids back during the Dark Ages, and no one knew at the time that they spawned in the banks of rivers or in spawning pits in the sand of slow-moving rivers or lakes. For some reason, I decided to go all out and pack the tank with nothing but rocks and no sand at all. My cichlids still managed to spawn for me! They made the best of the bad situation by placing the eggs in a depression in one of the rocks. The reader can imagine my surprise to see the pair fanning non-adhesive eggs, looking for all the world like gold nuggets, except that they bounced around a bit from the fanning actions.

The best way to get a pair is to get juveniles and raise them up. That way they will pair off naturally and non-violently. If you have no choice but to start with a pair of adults, make sure first that you have a pair. Then try keeping a glass barrier between the pair. They can court through the glass. If you time your release correctly, all will go well. It may even be that them will spawn with the glass between them and the eggs will be fertilized! It has happened many times. The male apparently gets close enough and times his ejection of sperm properly, and the water circulation does the rest.

All Central American cichlid fry are big enough to take newly hatched live brine shrimp once they are free swimming. That food should be supplemented with fine dry food. The fact is that most of the parents chew up food, ejecting it into the swarm of fry. And, remember, they get the supplemental food from the sides of their parents, too.

When you remove the fry from the pair, it is best to separate the parents. Remember that in the wild they would separate anyway. Males, being males, are always looking for a female to spawn again. If she is not willing she is driven away. In the aquarium, of course, the female can't leave. Hence there are many cases of spousal abuse by male cichlids because of ignorant cichlid owners. Here is a case of how knowing the natural history of a species and its method of spawning in nature helps us to avert possible tragedies.

Another thing to keep in mind is not to leave the fry in with the parents too long. As the fry grow, they continue to feed off the parents. In nature, they would have dispersed, or the parents could leave them. But in the aquarium such is not the case, and I have seen more than one parental cichlid in a pitiful state because its own young had cannibalized it to some degree. The parents are inhibited by their nature from eating the young in self-protection, so they have only a knowledgeable aquarist to keep a watchful eye on the situation.

There are those who hatch out the eggs artificially, but I am not even going to give directions for doing that. Although cichlids are often beautiful, their greatest charm is in the care they give their young. Also, studies have shown that the young grow better when left with the parents anyway, so why not leave them so that you can enjoy that never-tiring sight of cichlids tending their young? There is another factor involved. If all Central American cichlids are hatched artificially, we are not selecting out the bad parents, and the aquarium population of a given species may lose the very behavior that once made them so popular. (I must confess that with so many countless years of evolution, it would probably take a long time for genetic drift to eliminate good parental behavior, but I'm still against the artificial hatching of eggs.)

While it is true that cichlids spawn themselves, they must have certain resources for doing so. They must have good health and good nutrition. They must have a mate, and they must have a tank that gives them the feeling that they can successfully spawn and raise the young. Proper filtration, aquarium practices, and nutrition will provide the first prerequisite. Proper selection of fish and mixing procedures will provide the second. And a properly set up tank that is large enough, with lots of rockwork, will complete the picture. Unlike other keepers of fish, cichlid keepers nearly always attempt to spawn their charges. And why not? It is half the fun of keeping cichlids. Perhaps even more than that!

The beauty of some of the Central American species like this *Cichlasoma salvini* is just a small part of the rewards of keeping cichlids; watching the interactions between the parents and between the parents and their young would make the keeping of these fishes worthwhile even if they were completely drab.

THE GUIDE TO OWNING CENTRAL AMERICAN CICHLIDS

The male member of a pair of firemouth cichlids approaching his firemouthiest best (flaring his branchiostegal membranes, if you want to get technical about it) in warning an intruder not to mess with his babies.

# Index

# Photo Credits